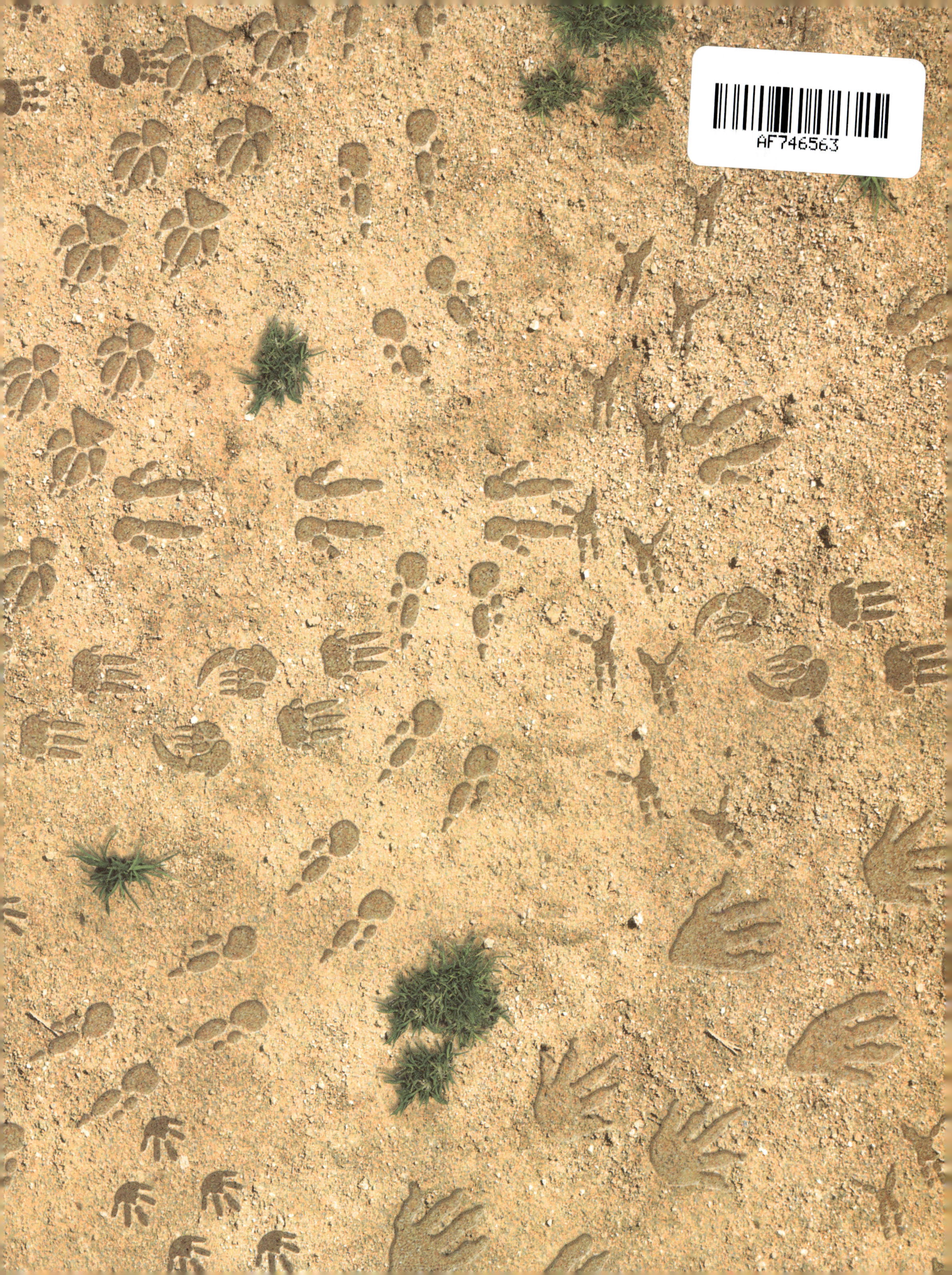

AUSTRALIA'S REMARKABLE WILDLIFE

JOHN LESLEY

COCKATOO

REDBACK publishing

First Published 2023 by
Redback Publishing
PO Box 357 Frenchs Forest NSW 2086
Australia

www.redbackpublishing.com
orders@redbackpublishing.com

Reprinted 2024

ISBN 978-1-925860-01-6 HBK

Author: John Lesley
Editor: Caroline Thomas
Design: Redback Publishing

NATIONAL LIBRARY OF AUSTRALIA
A catalogue record for this book is available from the National Library of Australia

Originated by Redback Publishing

Printed and bound in Malaysia

Acknowledgements
Abbreviations: l—left, r—right, b—bottom, t—top, c—centre, m—middle
We would like to thank the following for permission to reproduce photographs: (Images © shutterstock) p25tl Osprey Creative / Shutterstock.com

CONTENTS

SULPHUR-CRESTED COCKATOO

The sulphur-crested cockatoo has white body feathers and a crest of bright, yellow feathers on its head. When it is angry or ready to defend itself, it raises the crest to make itself look bigger.

Bare skin around eye

Yellow crest

Strong claws

Curved beak

COCKATOO BASIC FACTS

APPEARANCE

Sulphur-crested cockatoos are large, heavy birds. They grow to over half a metre long and can weigh more than a kilogram. They have a powerful, curved beak and strong claws. The claws are adapted for perching, but cockatoos also use them to hold food and even open garbage bin lids! Some cockatoos spend a lot of time on the ground looking for food. Their sharp claws are not a great adaptation for this activity, and cockatoos waddle, swaying from side to side as they walk.

NAME

The word cockatoo comes from a Malay word, kakatua. This became the Dutch word, kaketoe in the 1700s.

Cockatoos are parrots. There are several types of cockatoo living across Australia, and in Indonesia, Papua New Guinea, and other islands in the South Pacific and Southeast Asia.

The scientific name for the sulphur-crested cockatoo is *Cacatua galerita*.

COCKATOO ADAPTATIONS

Cockatoo fossils are rare, but scientists have found one at Riversleigh in Australia. It is about twenty million years old, showing that cockatoos have been around for much longer than people.

Sulphur-crested cockatoos have evolved over millions of years and have adapted to their environment in many ways. Like all birds, their ancient ancestors were dinosaurs.

FEATHERS

Cockatoos produce their own powder to keep their feathers in good condition. They rub this powder off their lower back and spread it around their feathers.

FLOCKS

Sulphur-crested cockatoos can live in flocks of hundreds of birds. Any predator would think twice about attacking a large flock of angry cockatoos with hundreds of dangerous beaks ready to bite.

COMMUNICATING

They have a range of sounds that help them either bond with other cockatoos or tell them they are ready to fight. Squawks, screeches and softer noises all mean different things.

CLAWS

The claws have two toes at the front and two at the back. This makes the foot ideal for holding and moving things, as well as for hanging upside down on wire.

BEAKS

The curved beak is extremely strong. It can break open seed pods that no other animal in the Australian bush can get at. The beak is also a weapon to use against predators.

COCKATOO HABITAT

Cockatoos live in the wooded regions of Australia, and in suburbs that have lots of trees and nature reserves.

Sulphur-crested cockatoos need to live in places that have old trees with hollows in them. They build their nests in these hollows. They defend the opening of the tree hollow from eagles and goannas that can reach the tops of trees and like to eat the eggs and chicks.

Cockatoos also nest in holes in the sides of rock faces. Sulphur-crested cockatoos have learned to interact with people. They gather in large numbers near farms and in the outer suburbs of cities, where they eat seeds, crops and garbage.

Their cleverness allows them to adapt to living in the habitat where they can find the most food.

COCKATOO LIFE CYCLE

A breeding pair of male and female sulphur-crested cockatoos will stay together for life. They are mature when they are about six years old.

Both parents make the nest in a tree hollow or even a hole in a rock wall. They line the nest with grass, bark and leaves.

A breeding pair will stay together for life

Baby cockatiel being handfed

The female lays one to three eggs. The male and female share sitting on the eggs and raising the chicks.

The chicks hatch after a month, covered in yellow down. They can fly and look after themselves after about two months.

If there is enough food in their environment, the young birds will stay with the parents. Many of the birds in large flocks may be related to each other.

In zoos and captivity, sulphur-crested cockatoos have lived for over seventy years.

COCKATOO FOOD CHAIN

WHAT EATS COCKATOOS?

Predators of cockatoos include goannas, snakes, eagles and hawks. On the ground, an unwary cockatoo can be taken by a cat or dog.

When they are feeding on the ground in flocks, one cockatoo stays up high in a tree to look out for danger. If they see a predator, they squawk, and the whole flock knows to fly away quickly.

WHAT DOES A COCKATOO EAT?

Cockatoos eat seeds, nuts and plant roots. They also enjoy eating grubs and insects, especially when they are producing their chicks and they need more protein.

PEOPLE AND COCKATOOS

PETS

People around the world love having cockatoos as pets. Unfortunately, this leads to the cruel and illegal export of wild birds from Australia. Pets should only be obtained from breeders who have raised the birds from chicks and treat them well.

HABITAT

The main threat to cockatoos is the destruction of their habitat. They need forests for food and for tree hollows for nests. Removing trees to make room for houses, businesses and roads means that there is less habitat for cockatoos.

PSITTACOSIS

Cockatoos can get an illness called psittacosis, which they can pass to humans.

This illness affects the lungs and makes both birds and people very sick.

PROTECTED

The behaviour of sulphur-crested cockatoos can result in expensive damage to properties and crops. Because of this, in some places in Australia, they can be killed or moved away. This can only occur under very strict conditions. Any harm caused to them otherwise can result in severe legal penalties.

OTHER COCKATOOS

Although the sulphur-crested cockatoo is the type most often seen around towns and cities on the east coast of Australia, there are also other types of cockatoo that live in the forest and on the grassy plains.

BLACK COCKATOOS:

GLOSSY BLACK COCKATOO

- Lives in forests in the eastern states of Australia
- Red tail feathers
- Female has yellow cheek feathers

YELLOW-TAILED BLACK COCKATOO

- Yellow cheek patches and yellow tail feathers
- Lives mostly in the eastern coastal forests of Australia

LONG-BILLED COCKATOO

- Found only in Western Australia
- Small crest
- Black feather with white edges
- Female has white cheeks

PALM COCKATOO

- Lives at the far north of Australia on the Cape York Peninsula
- Black crest
- Red cheeks
- Grows up to 60 cm long

CARNABY'S BLACK COCKATOO

- Lives in the southwest of Australia
- Has a small crest
- Black feathers with white bands under the tail feathers
- Declining in numbers due to the loss of its forest habitat

RED-TAILED BLACK COCKATOO

- Lives in eucalypt forests throughout Australia
- Male bird has bright red tail feathers

CORELLAS:

LITTLE CORELLA
WESTERN CORELLA
LONG-BILLED CORELLA

The three types of corella look similar to each other, but with some differences in size and colouring:

- White body with pink feathers around the face
- Found throughout most of Australia in towns and on farmland
- Need to have a source of water
- Form large flocks
- Need tree hollows for nesting
- Eat mainly seeds and fruit

Long-billed corella

SMALLEST COCKATOO:

COCKATIEL

The cockatiel is a small bird, growing to about 30 centimetres long. The body feathers are grey, with a yellow crest and orange cheek patches. White feathered cockatiels have been bred in captivity to satisfy the high demand for these birds as pets.

CANBERRA'S OWN BIRD:

GANG-GANG COCKATOO

This grey cockatoo is the bird emblem for the Australian Capital Territory. The male has red feathers on his face and a red crest.

Gang-gang cockatoo

PINK COCKATOOS:

MAJOR MITCHELL'S COCKATOO

Lives in the western arid areas of Australia, although it does need access to water, and to have trees for nesting. It has pink and white feathers, and a crest with bands of red and yellow.

GALAH

Galahs live throughout Australia. They are small cockatoos, with pink body feathers and a white head. They form enormous flocks in the wild but are usually only seen as pairs in suburban areas.

Major Mitchell's cockatoo

Galah

COCKATOOS ON THE 'RED LIST'

Some types of cockatoo exist in large populations and are not under any threat of extinction. Others are very vulnerable and could disappear in the future.

The International Union for Conservation of Nature (IUCN) Red List of Threatened Species is a list that shows whether an animal or plant is under threat of extinction.

Red-tailed black cockatoo

COCKATOO	ENDANGERED STATUS	NUMBERS IN THE WILD
Sulphur-crested cockatoo	✓	↓
Short-billed black cockatoo (Carnaby's black cockatoo)	X	↓
Long-billed black cockatoo	X	↓
Glossy black cockatoo	✓	↓
Red-tailed black cockatoo	✓	↓
Yellow-tailed black cockatoo	✓	~
Palm cockatoo	✓	↓
Galah	✓	↑
Western corella	✓	↑
Little corella	✓	↑
Long-billed corella	✓	↑
Gang-gang cockatoo	✓	↑
Major Mitchell's Cockatoo	✓	~
Cockatiel	✓	↑

X = Endangered
✓ = Not endangered

↓ = Decreasing
~ = Stable
↑ = Increasing

COCKATOO QUESTIONS AND ANSWERS

Q.

Why do sulphur-crested cockatoos damage buildings?

A.

Their beaks keep growing so they need to keep biting on something hard to stop the beak getting too long. In the wild, they bite hard wood. In suburban areas, where there are no old trees, they use the wood in houses instead.

Q.

Can I have a pet cockatoo?

A.

As with all Australian native wildlife, it is illegal to take a cockatoo from the wild. Pet cockatoos are raised by professional breeders. These are the only sources from which you should get a pet cockatoo.

Q.

Can they talk?

A.

Cockatoos make a lot of sounds to each other. Pet cockatoos learn to mimic the words humans say to them. It sounds like they are talking, but they are just making sounds.

Q.

Are they just playing?

A.

If you watch a cockatoo destroying a window frame, it looks as though they are just having fun. Like all the more intelligent animals, including us, cockatoos do seem to like to play.

SORTING ANIMALS INTO GROUPS

Biologists divide all living things around the world into groups. They call this process classification.

The two basic groups of animals are called:

VERTEBRATES

Vertebrates have a backbone

INVERTEBRATES

Invertebrates do not have a backbone

Vertebrates are further divided into these groups (classes). Cockatoos are birds and belong in the class called Aves.

FISH

AMPHIBIANS (AMPHIBIA)

REPTILES (REPTILIA)

BIRDS (AVES)

MAMMALS (MAMMALIA)

GLOSSARY

bond with make a connection with
captivity condition of not being free
crest feathers on top of head that stand up
down soft, fluffy feathers
fossil prehistoric remains of animals in old rocks
goanna large Australian reptile
interact have contact with
penalties punishments
predator animal that eats another animal
psittacosis parrot disease
vulnerable easily harmed

Palm cockatoo

4K UHD
00:35:02

4K UHD
00:35:02

4K UHD
00:35:02

INDEX